The heart of the mountains

In the heart of the ancient mountains of Eryri (*Snowdonia*), a warm welcome and an array of leisure activities await the holidaymaker. This is one of Wales' main tourist areas, attracting fans from all over Europe and beyond. The Romans were here in their time, and legends of ancient Welsh heroes are associated with many a peak, lake and crag. The industrial heritage of the *ardal* (locality) is extremely interesting from both a visual and social perspective.

According to one of the ancient *Trioedd Ynys Prydain* (Welsh triadic sayings), all one needs is 'an eye to see nature, a heart to feel nature and the resolve to follow nature'. Adherence to that particular wisdom would ensure a very pleasurable experience for anyone visiting this *ardal*. According to one traveller who was here in 1839, this place was created by nature on a holy day!

Wherever we go in Eryri – to the remotest *cymoedd* (pl. of *cwm*: corrie, valley) in the rocky embrace of the mountains, to the lakes of Yr Wyddfa (*Snowdon*), or to its panoramic peaks – it will always be in the company of seagulls. Wales' highest mountains are just a few kilometres from the its beaches – as the gull flies. And it was from the sea and the coast that the first settlers came.

There are few extant remains of these early inhabitants but maps show several *carneddi* (tumuli) and *cromlechi* (burial chambers) in the foothills of Eryri. The oldest dwellings in the *ardal* are the huts which were home to the indigenous peoples of the Bronze Age right up until the Middle Ages. In north-western Wales, the local name given to them is *cytiau'r Gwyddelod* (the Irish huts). These early houses consisted of low circular stone walls with a conical wooden frame supporting a straw or reed thatch. Several such dwellings have been reconstructed in museums throughout Wales [e.g. the St Fagan Museum of Welsh Life and Castell Henllys (Pembs.)].

In the parish of Llanddeiniolen, near Llanberis, is the site of a fortified village which was one of the *ardal*'s main defences, Dinas Dinorwig. The walls at the entrance are 4.6 metres thick, and deep ditches surround a hill above the Seiont valley. It is a prominent location within sight of several other Celtic forts along the north Wales coast, Tre'r Ceiri, Dinas Dinlle, Penmaen-mawr, Y Gogarth and Holyhead. The Celts settled from 500 BC, building a considerable number of hill forts, which even today remind us of the fortified hill-top villages of southern France, Italy and Spain.

'Dinas' was the Celtic word for a hill fort, (in modern Welsh it means 'city') and there are several examples in the area such as Dinas Tŷ Du which occupies a splendid defensive position to the west of Llanberis, and Dinas Mot and Dinas y Gromlech at Nant Peris.

Of all the different cultures which have come to the mountains of Eryri, it is the Celtic influence which is still most strongly felt. The Welsh language spoken here today derives from the language of the ancient Brythonic Celts who used to inhabit Dinas Dinorwig and the round huts which are to be found along the hillsides. The way of life here has changed several times since then, and yet much of the Celtic imagination still survives here and the old Celtic legends have been passed on from generation to generation.

Several legends have grown in an attempt to explain some of the more unusual rock formations in the vicinity. At the bottom of Bwlch Llanberis (the Llanberis pass) is the bridge called Pont y Gromlech where there is a place to park cars beside three enormous boulders. This, according to the legend, is the old *cromlech*, where Celtic heroes were buried and when there was talk of blowing them up to build a road, there was such an outcry from local people that the authorities were obliged to alter their plan and create a bed for the road between the *cromlech* and the river.

Dinas Dinorwig

Dinas y Gromlech

PENDINAS

D riving roads through the mountains has presented challenges to engineers over the centuries and Nant Peris and Bwlch Llanberis were to remain exceptionally remote until some two hundred years ago. No one managed to build a modern road through the pass until the beginning of 19th century.

But the Romans had no such problems. Their main fortress in north-western Wales was at Segontium on the edge of modern-day Caernarfon and they had a temporary fort at Penygwryd, near the present-day reservoir. It is possible to trace many of their roads through the mountains of Eryri.

The mist descends rapidly sometimes in these narrow valleys and it's not surprising that stories of giants and *tylwyth teg* (fairy folk) abound. The longest rock climb in Wales is to be found beneath Bwlch y Saethau on the cliffs of Lliwedd, ascending a sheer 400m rock face. According to legend, it is here that King Arthur and the Knights of the Round Table lie sleeping, awaiting the call for them to save Wales once more from her enemies. There are many Arthurian legends in Wales – the historical Arthur was one of the predominant classic warrior figures in early Welsh poetry. He was the leader of the Brythonic Celts in a kingdom comprising southern Scotland, Cumbria and Yorkshire, the west of England, Devon and Cornwall and, of course, Wales.

The political equilibrium in the island of Britain was shattered with the departure of the Roman legions as their empire began to disintegrate around 400 AD. In the west the Irish invaded Gwynedd and Teutonic tribes came from the Low Countries, Denmark and

Germany to eastern England. The Brythons united under King Arthur and his horsemen at the end of the 5th century and, by all accounts, he defeated the Saxons on several occasions and maintained the eastern borders of Wales far further han they are today.

Wales is full of legends extolling the feats and strength of their heroic king, one of which is located here above Llanberis. At one time the whole land was being blighted by an angry giant called Rhita. Several brave men fought against him but perished. Rhita would then remove their beards and add them to his flowing, if rather hairy, cloak. Eventually, there was just one hole left in the cloak which required a king's beard – no less – to fill it. A challenge was issued to Arthur, the most powerful king in the world at that time. Arthur came to the foot of the mountain with his army. To avoid suffering among his own men, Arthur himself accepted the challenge to fight the giant. The dreadful din of mortal combat resounded in the mists that lay over the mountain filling the soldiers encamped below with dread. Eventually, Arthur came down the mountainside victorious. The giant's body was left at the summit. Each and every one of his soldiers climbed the mountain and slapped down a rock on the giant's body, and that is how the highest mountain in Wales was formed – *Gwyddfa Rhita Gawr* (The Burial Mound of Rhita Gawr), Yr Wyddfa, or *Snowdon* as it is also known.

5

Llyn Peris

*T*he two lakes on the floor of the valley are named after two saints from the age of the Celtic Church: Sant Peris and Sant Padarn: Llyn Peris is the higher of the two lakes and above it stands Nant Peris and the ancient church of Sant Peris. This was the *ardal*'s first social centre. During a later period, the focal point for the local populace moved to the new village of Llanberis, , named, yet again, after the old saint of the parish. The village of Llanberis stands on the shores of Llyn Padarn and not those of Llyn Peris!

When Christianity reached Wales, it was upheld by monks and saints – as opposed to the episcopal institutions prevalent in the Church of Rome. Nevertheless, the Celtic Church was recognised by Rome long before Austin was sent as a missionary to the 'island of the Saxon tribes' in England. The emphasis of the Celtic Church was on a simple way of life and the establishment of small *llannau* (sing. *llan*, lit. an enclosed piece of land) in locations which were often remote. One of these saints was Peris. Not a great deal is known about him other than that his feast day would be celebrated on 11th December. Sant Padarn established a tiny chapel at Llwyn Padarn between Mynydd Gwefru and the Victoria Hotel in Llanberis.

The saints would roam the land, visiting other *llannau* and spreading the Word. Sant Peris seems to have been quite a traveller as the old name for Bwlch Llanberis was Gorffwysfa Peris (Peris' Rest) (Gorffwysfa is the name of the hostel at the head of the pass to this day). Opposite the church in Nant Peris is the old well associated with the saint, in the

St Padarn's, Llanberis

garden of Ty'r Ffynnon (*well house*). Some of the walls around the well still remain, but, at one time, the whole well was housed in a small building a couple of metres high, with a circular seat set above the water. A pair of trout used to be kept in the well, a fresh pair being introduced on their demise. Lovers would go to the well and the sight of both fish together was deemed to be a good omen for them.

St Peris' church

Originally, the church of Sant Peris was typical of several old churches in Wales – a simple, rectangular building. But a north and south transept were added in the sixteenth century and two chapels in the 17th century resulting in its unique shape. The most striking feature of the church is the chancel screen dating from the early 1500s. Its design is simple, but rather beautiful, and perfect for its setting nestling in the mountains. To the left of the opening in the screen there is a wooden community chest with three locks on it. This is known as Cyff Peris (*cyff* = fund) and probably dates from the 17th century.

There are several interesting tombstones in the graveyard: one of which relates the sad tale of a little 7 year old boy called John Closs who got lost on the mountain in December 1808 and died in a snowstorm. The large church of Sant Padarn today stands in the middle of Llanberis – the present building dating from the Victorian era.

The Lakes

*T*he *ardal* is renowned for the splendour of the two lakes on the valley floor, their waters constantly reflecting the beauty of the surrounding mountains. But in the high *cymoedd*, there are several lakes which gleam like pearls in the shadow of the crags and they too are well worth a visit.

Llyn Padarn

A long narrow lake, 28.65 metres in depth at its deepest point. This is one of only three lakes in Eryri which contain *torgoch* (a native fish) as a natural species – some of them weighing over 450gm each. A local fishing club also stocks the lake with unfarmed trout. Rowing and canoeing are popular on the lake as well as trips on a pleasure boat from Parc Padarn. The rowing competitions for the 1958 Olympics were held on Llyn Padarn and an annual swimming competition is also takes place here.

Llyn Padarn over, winter

Llyn Peris

On the shores of Llyn Peris in 1974 work was begun on the largest pump-storage scheme in Europe. A network of tunnels were drilled through the mountain of Elidir Fawr so that the water could be released at short notice from Marchlyn Mawr to generate electricity through turbines embedded in the core of the mountain. Some 4283hl of water flows every second producing 1,300 megawatts of electricity in 10 seconds. The water is stored in Llyn Peris during the day and then at night is pumped back up the mountainside to Marchlyn Mawr while there is off-peak electricity available. Special steps were taken to protect the environment and, surprisingly enough, every species of fish has found its way back to the

llyn, despite it not having being restocked.

Llyn Llydaw This is a sheltered location at the foot of Yr Wyddfa. In contemplating its quiet waters, it will come as no surprise that Llyn Llydaw at 58.5m is one of Eryri's deepest lakes The remains of an old Celtic *crannog* have been found here – a village built on an island of wooden poles, using the water of the lake as a natural defence. The path from Gorffwysfa, crosses a causeway over the lake – when this was being built for the copper ore mill in 1853, an old log boat was discovered in the mud.

Glaslyn The green (*glas*) of copper ore is very obvious in the waters of this circular lake under the buttresses of Yr Wyddfa. A tale is told of an exceptionally strong – and bearded – woman who lived in this *cwm* – Cadi Cwm Glas. When one of the miners began to make fun of her because of her profusion of facial hair, Cadi held the unfortunate individual by his ankles over one of the leats running into the copper mill! There are also many legends and stories about *tylwyth teg* (fairy folk) associated with this lake.

Llyn Du'r Arddu *Du* (black/dark) is the predominant colour of the waters of this lake which is at the base of a cliff, Clogwyn Du'r Arddu, one of the most renowned rock faces in Wales for climbers.

Llyn Peris and Dolbadarn (Wilson)

Llyn Llydaw

Glaslyn (above) and Marchlyn Mawr

Castell Dolbadarn

*T*his castle, on the rock overlooking the meadow between the two lakes, together with Dolwyddelan castle, formed part of Eryri's defences, which succeeded on more than one occasion in enduring incursions by the kings of England into Gwynedd.

The old name for the site was Caer Peris, and it was subsequently called Castell Padarn. This is probably one of the oldest fortified defences in Wales – in the sixth century there was a fort here believed to have been given as a gift to Caradog, king of Cornwall, who brought an army to Wales to help Maelgwn Gwynedd defeat the English.

The existing castle was built around 1208 by Llywelyn Fawr to defend the route through Bwlch Llanberis. In contrast to Dolwyddelan castle, Dolbadarn has a round tower in the Norman style, and its romantic setting, with the crags of Eryri as a backdrop, has attracted artists for centuries.

Llywelyn Fawr was soon succeeded by Llywelyn ap Gruffudd. His road to kingship was a rocky one. In order to keep Gwynedd united, he was obliged, in 1255, to fight against his brothers Owain and Dafydd on the battlefield at Bryn Derwin above Clynnog. He captured Owain and imprisoned him in Dolbadarn castle until 1277. Llywelyn acquired the homage of all the Welsh lords – and even the English crown – assuming the title of *Tywysog Cymru* (Prince of Wales) for the first time ever. Edward I was not one to keep his word, however, and when he got his second wind, he spent enormous sums of money raising huge armies to invade Wales. Llywelyn was killed in an ambush at Cilmeri (near Llanfair-ym-Muallt (Builth)) in 1282 where a memorial stone refers to him as *Ein Llyw Olaf*

– our last prince.

Dolbadarn was the final refuge of the last of the independent princes of Gwynedd. Dafydd, Llywelyn's brother, took advantage of its powerful location in 1283, before being forced to escape into the mountains, where he was captured and eventually barbarically executed on the streets of Shrewsbury.

Edward I drew up plans for a chain of castles along the shores of Eryri – powerful strongholds which could be supplied from the sea. He had no desire to maintain mountain castles such as Dolbadarn and Dolwyddelan – they were castles to protect the lands of the indigenous people. Caernarfon, Conwy and the rest of the Norman castles were built to protect the oppressors. In many ways, a simple, primitive castle such as Dolbadarn is much more interesting and has about it a certain dignity and strength. Edward's castles were showpieces, but at the same time they bore testimony to the fear and respect which the invaders had for the Welsh and their leaders.

At the time of the Glyndŵr rebellion, Owain Glyndŵr's arch-enemy – Lord Grey – was imprisoned at Dolbadarn. The castle returned to Welsh hands in 1488 when a lease was procured by Maredudd ap Ieuan. It became part of the Faenol Estate in 1627 coming into public ownership in 1941. Nowadays, it is Cadw, the organisation responsible for historical monuments in Wales, which preserves its history.

Lili'r Wyddf

Edward Llw

A visit to Eryri involves not only stunning views of the mountains and *cymoedd*, but also a chance to discover a unique and species-rich natural world. Over the centuries the variety of plants and flowers in this *ardal* has attracted many naturalists.

Welsh folk literature and memory go back to the time of the Celtic druids and many traditional herbal remedies have been passed on from generation to generation. Identifying and studying the local flora was part of our heritage and there would be skilled herbalists in every *bro* (neighbourhood). The first recorded visit by a herbalist from outside the area was Thomas Johnson, an apothecary from London who came here in the company of Thomas Glyn, Glynllifon in August 1639. Although that was not really the best month for finding alpine plants, Johnson recorded in his journal that he collected a significant number of the rare plants for which Eryri was famed.

From a Welsh perspective, however, the most influential naturalist to visit the *ardal* on several occasions was Edward Llwyd (1660-1709). Hans Sloan, the President of the Royal Society, referred to him as 'the best naturalist in Europe at present', and he is considered to be one of the most versatile Welshmen ever – he was a scholar, a naturalist, an archaeologist, and a traveller.

At the top of the Welsh botanical charts is *Lili'r Wyddfa (Lloydia serotina)*, a small insignificant little plant with thin reedy leaves and white flowers with a green stripe along each petal. It only flowers for a short time – about a fortnight at the beginning of June. The

Ceunant Mawr's glen

plant was discovered by Edward Llwyd in 1690, and was named in Latin in his honour. This is the rarest alpine plant on the island of Britain and is only to be found in some 5 or 6 locations in Eryri.

During the Victorian era, ferns became a great source of interest and consequently botanists began swarming over the rocks of Eryri in search of them. The tragedy is that several species of rare fern were taken from their natural habitat to gardens and greenhouses over the border. Some species were totally wiped out while only a few specimens of others were left on inaccessible cliffs beyond the clutches of collectors.

Despite these losses, conservation is now the watchword, and if the rarest plants are out of reach, there are plenty of other specimens to attract and amaze the naturalists who come here. There is probably no other area like it throughout the island of Britain and the remarkable botany of Eryri is a subject which could fill any number of volumes. The observant rambler is sure to find several unusual specimens on the most accessible tracks, but the lesson, hopefully, has now been learnt – in order to continue to enjoy them, none of these plants should ever be lifted.

(above) Purple saxifrage

W hen the native Welsh princes and nobility lost their power, a new generation of landowners emerged who did not shy from seizing land and riches at every possible opportunity. One of the largest estates in northern Wales was the Faenol Estate. At its zenith, it stretched over 15441ha, encompassing some 27 parishes from Dyffryn Conwy to Llŷn.

The origins of the estate are to be found in the old *maenor* of Dinorwig which was leased to Thomas Williams, Cochwillian in the 16th century after his father fought with Henry Tudor in the battle of Bosworth. Towards the end of Elizabeth's reign, a new house was built which is now in an increasingly dilapidated condition, but there is hope that it will be restored to its former glory.

The old Welsh family, who were patrons to poets and who maintained vestiges of the old traditions, died out and the estate fell into the hands of John Smith from Tedworth, the Speaker of the House of Commons and subsequently to Thomas Assheton Smith from Cheshire. For almost a century, the estate was neglected by absentee landlords but it became a little more prosperous when Assheton Smith began opening up slate quarries and stealing the *Tir Comin* (Common Land) from the local communities.

The *Tir Comin* had been divided between the whole community for over a thousand years under the Welsh laws of Hywel Dda, but Assheton Smith and another landowner insisted on pushing an Enclosure Act through Parliament in their own interests.

(above) A musical festival is held at the Faenol every August

There is an old Welsh saying: 'you can be hanged for stealing a sheep from the mountain, but you can be made a lord for stealing the mountain itself,' and this was indeed the case in this *ardal*. A number of quarrymen and smallholders who had built cottages on the *Tir Comin* were to be evicted. The squatters organised a meeting which became unruly, and the authorities read out the Riot Act. Without lawyers to fight their case, several of the *Tir Comin* tenants were thrown into Caernarfon gaol.

The main Agent of the Faenol Estate, John Evans, was very forceful in his actions against the smallholders. When he returned with the Justice of the Peace and several constables to break up their dwellings, the crowd went berserk and soldiers had to be called. The quarrymen left their work to join the ranks of the smallholders in an attempt to save their homes. A fire was lit in one of the cottages and a cauldron of water was boiled to be thrown over John Evans who was also pelted with mud and clods of earth.

His suit was ruined and his pride dented, but a number of the smallholders were arrested and soldiers arrived to protect Assheton Smith's property. A total of 1554ha were enclosed, with some 1059ha of this being allocated to Assheton Smith. He was the local Member of Parliament at the time.

The new mansion of the Faenol...

...and an old cottage at Fach-wen

I t is impossible to escape the quarry in Llanberis. Quarrying is a very wasteful industry. Ten tonnes of waste are produced for every tonne of slate and more than half the slopes of Elidir Fawr have been scarred by slate works. Two centuries of working the *ponciau* (levels or galleries) has thrown up huge spoil tips above the eastern side of Llyn Peris. The quarry shut down suddenly, but not unexpectedly, in 1969.

Slates have been sheared from the rocks of northern Wales for over 1,800 years – slate was used in the Roman fort at Segontium and the Norman castle at Conwy. In the eighteenth century, slates were mined for private use in this *ardal*, but that was curtailed by Assheton Smith when he enclosed the *Tir Comin*. In 1809, he formed his own company and began to develop the industry on a large scale.

Originally, slates were transported by boat across the lake to Penllyn, Cwm y Glo and from there they were taken in carts to Caernarfon. By 1848-1849, the quarry company had built a railway to transport materials directly from the workshops to the harbour at Y Felinheli. From there, they would be exported all over the world. Nearly 5,600 tonnes of Dinorwig slate went to Australia in 1882 alone, a year which saw Welsh slate quarries producing over a quarter of a million tonnes of slate. Slate was utilised in several other ways apart from as a roofing material – gravestones, hearths, billiard tables and telephone switchboards on large ships. But obviously, the greatest demand was for roofing slates – in particular as the Industrial Revolution saw whole new areas being

populated almost overnight, and as emigrants established their townships and cities in the New World.

In its heyday, the quarry was a self-sufficient world, with its own barracks to accommodate the workers who would stay there during the week. From Llanberis, you can see the ponciau or terraced galleries, which the quarrymen would work, each *ponc* with its own name, such as 'Abyssinia', 'California', 'Twll Mwg' (*smoke hole*) or 'Aberdaron'.

Working under arduous conditions in all weathers and *yn nannedd y graig* (in the teeth of the rock face) led inevitably to frequent accidents at the quarry, many of which were fatal. In 1860, a hospital was built with its own doctor and operating theatre as part of the quarry. This is now open to the public, showing the beds of the unfortunate inmates and the apparatus used – including a wooden leg which would be lent out to any unfortunate amputee until he had purchased his own. A shilling (5p) would be docked from the quarrymen's wages to run the hospital.

Over the years, a number of machines were introduced which facilitated the heavy work, but, to this day, the slate still has to be split by hand. This is a craft which relies on human talent, which, together with the quarrymen's skills and the nature of the rock, ensured that Welsh slates were the very best in the world.

Gilfach Ddu Slate Museum

The work and life of the quarrymen of northern Wales have been preserved and wonderfully presented at the Slate Museum in Y Gilfach Ddu in the Padarn Country Park. A good way to begin a visit is to watch the 3D audio-visual film 'Stealing the Mountain', which provides a background and extracts from the history of Dinorwig quarry and the society which grew up around the slate industry.

The workshop at Y Gilfach Ddu serviced all the requirements of the quarry, as well as those of the trains and ships. There are over 80km of railway tracks in the quarry itself, not to mention the narrow gauge line down to Y Felinheli. A visit to the workshops, the machine shop, the smithy and the iron and brass foundry, shows just how self-sufficient the quarry was. The workers used to boast that they could repair anything that a quarry might need – from sharpening a chisel to making a steam engine. A quick tour of the foundry and the template store soon confirms this.

The templates were all made of wood and all of them – over 2,000 in number – have been preserved. Some of them are exceptionally complex and meticulously crafted, with the finest details being carved by hand. The craftsmen would apprentice each other, and very often son would follow father in his craft, and so it is not surprising that whole families would be known by the nickname *'Patrwm'* (template) in Llanberis.

Every now and then, the foundry is fired and there is an opportunity for visitors to see metal being turned into molten liquid and poured white hot into templates in the beds of

sand. Another striking feature in the museum is the big water wheel which supplied power to all the workshops between 1870 and 1925. This was the largest industrial wheel in Wales.

The quarry's main arteries were the inclines which carried the rocks from the different levels. The weight of the full wagons was used to raise the empty wagons back to the top of the slope. You can see craftsmen still engaged in the old craft of *hollti* (splitting) and *naddu* (chipping) in Y Gilfach Ddu.

In 1998, a terrace of houses from Tanygrisiau near Blaenau Ffestiniog were moved to Y Gilfach Ddu. Every stone, slate and beam was numbered and subsequently re-erected in their entirety, care being taken with every detail. The houses have now been furnished to convey the three periods in the quarry's history. 1861, the industry's golden age; 1901, the time of the strike at the Penrhyn Quarry in Bethesda, a dispute which lasted three years, creating a deep rift in the quarrying community of that town (see the warning in the window 'No scabs in this house.'); the final house in the terrace recreates the atmosphere in 1969, the year Chwarel Dinorwig was closed.

The popular 'Caffi'r Ffowntan', which is renowned for its traditional Welsh home cooking, is another attraction to the museum.

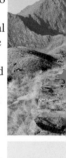

oday there are very few obvious remains to draw visitors' attention to the importance of copper mining in Eryri. Nevertheless, several generations ago, it was a major industry. There are still some traces to be seen, however – old shafts on the hillsides, the disused barracks and mills as well as a few odd bits of machinery. The presence of copper ore in the rock is what gives the clear blue-green hue to some of the lakes in the area. The name 'Glaslyn' for example, literally means 'blue/green lake'.

One of the earliest mines above Nant Peris employed between 40 and 50 men. As you walk towards the summit of Yr Wyddfa from Bwlch Gorffwysfa (Pen-y-pas), one option is to follow the Miner's Track. This goes past the old workers' barracks at Llyn Teyrn, the copper mill at Llyn Llydaw and ascends to the old workings at Glaslyn which are almost six hundred metres above sea level. It is difficult to imagine the deafening cacophany of blasting and milling which would have filled the air among these crags some two hundred years ago. Buckets on a wire ropeway and tramways would bring the ore down from the mountain.

The working conditions, of course, were very arduous in this type of terrain. Only during the summer months was it possible to work some of the highest shafts such as those at Clogwyn Coch near Llyn Du'r Arddu. During the hardest months, the miners would get an extra blanket in the barracks! The winter of 1801 was exceptionally hard when a tunnel had to be cut through the snow to reach the level, as the drifts were some 18 metres deep in places. Women and children were employed in the mill to break the ore with hammers before

it was taken to ships from Swansea moored at tCaernarfon.

The journey to Bwlch y Gorffwysfa along the A4086 down to the harbour is easy enough these days – but that was not the case two centuries ago. The Caernarfon road came to an end at the big rock in Cwm y Glo and there was nothing for it but to use ponies along the mountain track – Lôn Clegir – or else take a boat along the lakes to Nant Peris. As was the case with the earliest slates, the copper would be transported by boat down the mountain to Cwm y Glo.

In the second half of the 18th century a woman called Margiad uch Ifan lived in Penllyn. She was a bit of an Amazon, and renowned for her strength and was the chief oarswoman on the boats which brought the ore across the lake. Moreover she built her own boats, would go hunting with the best huntsmen in Eryri and could shoe horses. An old Welsh song lists her accomplishments and it is said that she was 102 when she died in 1789.

At the outset, the mine workings were very productive – one miner called Siôn John Roberts spotted a good vein of copper and was able to earn himself £300 in 3 months. Today, the drilling and blasting, the hammering and the milling have come to an end – but there are many kilometres of shafts and huge underground chambers which remain in the mountains as testimony to the industrious nature of these tough old miners.

Llanberis – the 'new' village

With the growth of the quarry, a 'new' village was developed at Llanberis. In its heyday, the slate industry employed some 3,000 workers in the *ardal* and however hard the work and low the wages might have been, they were much higher than rural wages in general at that time. There was a demand for housing and shops and other services and Llanberis grew to be one of the most important villages in the county. In addition, the tourist industry had begun to establish itself and a number of hotels were built there.

Once again, it was Thomas Assheton Smith, Y Faenol, who was the first to see the niche in the market for tourism. In 1830, he built the Victoria Hotel on the edge of the village. The road through Bwlch Llanberis was built in 1831 which made things easier for travellers to access the region. In 1869, the LNWR railway company opened the route from Caernarfon, establishing a station on the site occupied by Mynydd Gwefru (Electric Mountain) today.

Although the slate industry produced considerable profits for the owners, very little of that was seen by the quarrymen themselves. Attempts were made during the 19th century to establish a trade union in the north Wales quarries. The quarrymen of Glyn Rhonwy to the north of Llanberis were the first to ensure union recognition by an owner.

In order to prevent trade unionism from spreading any further, the owners tried to stop the quarrymen from meeting – not only in the quarry but also on any piece of land which was owned by the Faenol estate. At the far end of Llyn Padarn there is a rock which forms a natural amphitheatre standing on the old estate

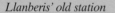
Llanberis' old station

of Lord Newborough of Glynllifon. The quarrymen of the area began to meet in the shadow of the rock and it has become known ever since as 'Craig yr Undeb' (*union rock*). In 1974, hundreds of people gathered at the rock to celebrate the centenary of the founding of the North Wales Quarrymen's Union under the leadership of Robert Parry, Ceunant, and a memorial plaque was put in place to mark the occasion.

438 people lived in Llanberis in 1811; the population had increased to 3014 by 1901. Old chapels were demolished and larger ones built in their place - the Methodist Capel Coch was established in 1777 and although it was rebuilt several times in granite, it kept its original name, the *coch* (red) referring to a much smaller edifice built of brick.

Chapels have always been important institutions in the quarrying areas and represent the self-determination of the workers in upholding their own religion. The chapels were also cultural centres running a whole range of musical and literary events which were a feature of the social life in the quarrying communities. 'Hogiau'r eglwys' (*the churchgoers*), on the other hand, was a pejorative term for the quarry stewards – sycophantic officials who crept up to the quarry owners. They traditionally would be affiliated to the same denominations as the big landed families.

Victoria Hotel

Capel Coch

An old wages' tin owned by a quarryman   23

It is said that you can see twenty lakes from the summit of Yr Wyddfa on a reasonably clear day. From the summit too, you can see a number of paths stretching like ribbons in the distance – paths which were created by generations of walkers heading for the summit from different directions. It is difficult to believe these days, but at one time, the mountain was devoid of tracks. Then travellers began to show an interest in climbing to the peak which led to the birth of 'Tywyswyr yr Wyddfa' or 'Snowdon Guides'.

Some of the early mountaineers had already experienced the romance of the Alps, and there was a great interest in botany. But without any paths, they had little choice but to hire local men who were familiar with the slopes. They were real characters and dressed in a particular way to attract attention.

One of the most renowned guides was 'Wil Boots' (William Williams, 1805-1861), a boot boy at the Victoria Hotel. He knew the whereabouts of the rare plants and ferns and this, combined with a considerable knowledge, led to him becoming known as the 'Botanical Guide' in order to distinguish him from the other guides. He accompanied several famous botanists who came to the *ardal* looking for plants. He died in an accident on Clogwyn y Garnedd.

Several of the earliest travellers came here because of upheavals in Europe which had placed restrictions on the traditional Grand Tour, but when they reached Eryri, the local inhabitants were suspicious of them because they spoke a strange language. They thought they were spies for Napoleon, but their

suspicions were allayed somewhat once they understood that the strange gabblings were English and not French!

As the tourist industry flourished, it became a tradition for anyone who came to northern Wales to make an attempt on the summit of Yr Wyddfa. Trips to the summit on the back of mules and ponies were organised from Llanberis along the more gradual path which leads from the village to the summit.

Saturday, 15 December, 1894, was an historical day indeed, for this was the date on which work commenced on building the narrow-gauge railway to the summit of Yr Wyddfa. This was the first funicular railway on the island of Britain. The line was opened officially on Easter Monday 1896. It is a remarkable railway journey – 8km in length, taking an hour to make the ascent and another hour to come back down, the engine having to travel extremely slowly during the ascent and descent. There were several serious accidents on the line during the early days, but for over a hundred years now, the old train has proved itself to be safer than walking the paths along the high rocky ridges.

With the paths laid down and the train running, the age of the old guides came to an end.

MOUNTAIN RAILWAY
LLANBERIS

PEN·Y·GWRYD
HOTEL

BAR   LUNCH

The Penygwryd Hotel was built in the 1830s and twenty years later, a new hotel was built on the old site of Gorffwysfa Peris at the top of Bwlch Llanberis. This was the era when experienced scramblers and climbers would come in droves to Eryri to tackle the challenging rock faces of Yr Wyddfa and Nant Peris. Much pioneering work in mountain craft was undertaken at that time and the names in the visitors' book at the Penygwryd Hotel are a veritable roll call of the top names in mountaineering in the island of Britain during the second half of the 19th century. The owner of the hotel organised a rescue team to search for climbers in distress. This honourable tradition continues.

Among those who have inscribed their names on the ceiling at Penygwryd are John Hunt and Charles Evans and other members of the first expedition to conquer Sargarmatha (*Everest*) in 1952. The entire team practised and trained here prior to facing the ultimate mountaineering challenge.

Local men also feature among those who developed the craft of conquering the crags. The rector of Llanberis and Llanrug, the Reverend Peter Bayley Williams was a pioneer in this respect, and when the renowned botanist, the Reverend William Bingley came to spend some time with him in 1798, it was this rather unlikely pair who made the the first recorded rock climb. They ascended Clogwyn Du'r Arddu whilst looking for rare alpine plants to plant in the rector's garden! Bingley described the climb: 'without once reflecting on the dangers involved: 'When he had fixed himself securely to a part of the rock, he took

off his belt and holding firmly by one end, gave the other to me . . . and with a little aid from the stone fairly pulled myself up by it'. According to G.A. Lister, this passage contains the germ of the concept of using a rope for climbing.

The mountains have caught the imagination of a large number of writers, artists, photographers and climbers. The tendency of some of the Victorian travellers, however, was to view the country as a personal playground, and their scribblings betray ignorance and inexperience. The mountains can be very dangerous places where the weather changes rapidly.

Today, however, there are plenty of opportunities to appreciate the risks involved and to learn how to avoid them, with information updates on the weather on the peaks available at the Llanberis Visitor Centre. The first national park on the island of Britain was established in Eryri in 1951, and gradually visitors have come to learn that it is not a park in the sense of somewhere to play in. Shepherds still go about their ancient craft on these mountains and the old way of life is protected here, just as much as the magnificent scenery.

As well as respecting paths and not leaving litter, the modern visitor has also learnt – in contrast to the old rector of Llanberis – that wild flowers look better in their natural habitat than in cultivated gardens!

MOUNTAIN MYNYDD GWEFRU

*T*he legendary giants and *tylwyth teg* of legend are not thin on the ground around Llanberis, but having visited Mynydd Gwefru (*Electric Mountain*), the visitor can really claim to have come face to face with a giant! This is the largest electricity pump-storage station in Europe, mostly hidden in the core of Elidir Fawr with the station itself located in the biggest man-made cavern in the world.

In creating this power station, the upper lake – Llyn Peris – was totally drained, so it could be deepened and enlarged. The lake contained the *torgoch*, a unique species of fish, which has remained unchanged since the last Ice Age. The fish were carefully netted and transported to other deep lakes in Eryri. Marchlyn Mawr high up on the slopes of Elidir was also enlarged. The water comes down from Marchlyn Mawr to turn the turbines in the mountain before being discharged into Llyn Peris. Then the same water is pumped back to Marchlyn Mawr to await the next urgent demand for electricity on the national grid.

Although the power station is in the heart of the mountain, under the old quarry, you can go in to see it and to wonder at the incredible feat of engineering which has made it possible.

The visit begins in the Mynydd Gwefru centre on the shores of Llyn Padarn near Llanberis. Here the technology is explained and there is an opportunity for children to get hands-on experience of producing their own electricity. Care has been taken to provide access and facilities for the disabled, in the building and throughout the tour. A minibus

will then take the party, accompanied by a guide, deep into the mountain to give them a taste of the 16km of tunnels and the extraordinary engineering involved.

When Llyn Peris was drained, an old clinker boat from the 16th century emerged from its depths. It had been lying in the silt on the bottom of the lake for 500 years. The boat was restored and, together with a dugout canoe from the 12th century, is displayed in a special room in the Mynydd Gwefru museum.

Supernatural legends are not just from the past in this *ardal*. Whilst work was being done on Marchlyn Mawr, a new folk legend sprang up. One day, some workers saw a huge dumper truck, with two men on board, slipping backwards into the lake and disappearing into the depths. Two men on the shore were quick-witted enough to leap into a boat in an attempt to save their fellow workers, but there was no sign of them. Suddenly, a huge gust of wind swept over the waters of the lake. The men were sucked out of the lorry and deposited in the boat!

It is not surprising in a *bro* which is so renowned for its legends, that new ones are still being created. Whether you believe them or not, the 'giant' still roars in Eryri and illuminates the land with his awesome lightning.

Something for everyone

Today, Parc Gwledig Padarn (*Padarn Country Park*) on the shores of Llyn Padarn offers a range of facilities and attractions amidst some of the most dramatic scenery in Eryri.

There are a number of theme trails which can be followed in the area. Llwybrau Bro'r Llechi (*the slate trails*) cut across the valley floor and lower slopes and follow in the footsteps of the old quarrymen as they made their way back and forth to work in all weathers. There are also paths which have been adapted for the disabled and for cyclists. The park itself extends over some 325ha, and contains two Sites of Special Scientific Interest – Coed Allt Wen and Llyn Padarn – as well as a local Nature Conservancy site. For those who enjoy a leisurely stroll, there is Llwybr Glas y Dorlan (*the kingfisher trail*), which leads from the main car park along the edge of the lake and this path has also been adapted for wheelchairs and pushchairs.

The Vivian Quarry also provides a chance to do some rock-climbing with ropes or to plumb the depths with diving gear. From here you can also visit the only incline in Wales which has been fully restored and is operational once more. Small sailing and rowing boats can be hired on the lake, or you can enjoy the scenery on board *Brenhines Eryri* and hear stories from the area's history.

In 1848, the owners of the Dinorwig Quarry built the narrow gauge railway for the quarry's use. Nowadays, the old locomotives still puff their way valiantly along the rails - the Llyn Padarn railway was extended so that it now runs from the village of Llanberis down to

Ras yr Wyddfa – the Snowdon race is an annual attraction

Penllyn and back! Once again, the views from the train cannot be seen from the car. On the return journey, the train stops at Cei Llydan. The passengers can get out and wander the woods at Y Fachwen and enjoy a quiet picnic or the adventure park facilities, before catching a later train back.

There are plenty of eating houses and cafés in the area – the slate museum, Llyn Padarn railway, Mynydd Gwefru and the railway to the summit of Yr Wyddfa all have good food and drink facilities and there are several cafés and restaurants in the village offering high quality refreshments. The village streets offer a range of shops and exhibitions for those who are looking for crafts and souvenirs of their visit to Llanberis. There are several slate craftsmen in the area – some of them ex-quarrymen, their skill in carving this hard rock into clocks, fans, garden sculpture or house name plates a constant source of admiration. There are quite o few local potteries too – some of which are open to the public – and jewellery makers, coppersmiths, artists, picture framers and reproduction print manufacturers, all provide entertaining displays and an opportunity to buy interesting and varied wares. All in all, a taste of the unique landscape and heritage of Llanberis will enrich your experience of Wales (see www.*visitsnowdonia.info*).

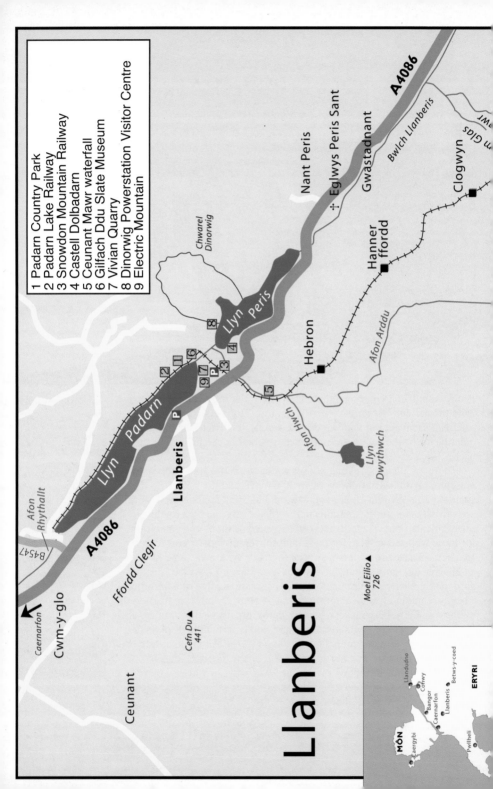

Llanberis

Key:
1 Padarn Country Park
2 Padarn Lake Railway
3 Snowdon Mountain Railway
4 Castell Dolbadarn
5 Ceunant Mawr waterfall
6 Gilfach Ddu Slate Museum
7 Vivian Quarry
8 Dinorwig Powerstation Visitor Centre
9 Electric Mountain

A4086

Afon Rhythallt

B4547

Caernarfon

Cwm-y-glo

Ceunant

Fford Clegir

Cefn Du ▲ 441

Llyn Padarn

Llanberis

Chwarel Dinorwig

Llyn Peris

Moel Eilio ▲ 726

Afon Hwch

Llyn Dwythwch

Hebron

Afon Arddu

Nant Peris

✝ Eglwys Peris Sant

Gwastadnant

Bwlch Llanberis

A4086

Hanner ffordd

Clogwyn

n Glas wr

MÔN
Caergybi
Llandudno
Conwy
Bangor
Caernarfon
Llanberis
Betws-y-coed
Pwllheli
ERYRI